BASKETBALL STORIES

FOR KIDS

Kevin Parker

© **Copyright Kevin Parker 2024 – All rights reserved.**

This book is copyright-protected. It is for personal use only. No part of this book may be reproduced, distributed, or transmitted in any form or by any means, including photocopying, recording, or other electronic or mechanical methods, without the prior written permission of the author.

The publisher and author will not be held liable for any damages, reparations, or financial losses resulting from the information in this book, whether directly or indirectly. You are solely responsible for your own decisions, actions, and their outcomes.

Disclaimer:

The stories in "Basketball Stories for Kids" are based on real events and people; however, some tales are products of fiction. Names, characters, businesses, places, events, locales, and incidents are either the products of the author's imagination or used in a fictitious manner. Any resemblance to actual persons, living or dead, or actual events is purely coincidental.

This book is intended for entertainment and educational purposes only. The content of this book should not be construed as professional advice or as a substitute for professional consultation.

The author has made every effort to ensure the accuracy of the information contained in this book, but certain details may be fictionalized or altered.

All trademarks, service marks, product names, and company names or logos appearing in this book are the property of their respective owners.

ISBN: 9798335017411 (Paperback)
ISBN: 9798335034661 (Hardcover)

TABLE OF CONTENTS

INTRODUCTION 5

CHAPTER 1. ESSENTIALS 6
When And Why Is the Basket? 6
3-Point Line Birthday 11
Basketball Language 16
It's Not Only About the Shoes 24
Jumpman Logo 30
The Greatest of All Time 34
NBA Nicknames 40

CHAPTER 2. INCREDIBLE FACT STORIES 45
13 Points In 33 Seconds 45
The Black Mamba Show 51
Unbeatable 100-Point Record 54
72 Win Games in One Season 58
11 Rings. Two Icons 62
The Most Underrated Players 74
Undrafted Players Who Became Champion 80
Cut From a School Team Becomes the Greatest 84

CHAPTER 3. INSPIRATIONAL TALES 88
Inside The Team 88
Role Models 94
Started From the Bottom, Now We Are Here 100

CHAPTER 4. MOTIVATION CHARGER 106
30 Motivational Quotes 106
Motivational Movies List 112

INTRODUCTION

This book is devoted to you and your favorite game. Here, you will find motivation and inspiration to fulfill your dreams.

You will become familiar with the history of the basketball game in the first chapter. The main episodes and the characters who build this history are in the second chapter. A third chapter is devoted to inspiring you with tales. And, in the fourth chapter, you will find a valuable list of motivational quotes and movies.

It's up to you what you want to read first. You can start even from the last chapter if you need to. And don't forget a pencil to highlight your favorite moments.

Also, at the very end, there is a practical surprise for you! You have there a place where you can write down your notes, dreams, and even a place to visualize them.

So, let's begin from the start ...

CHAPTER 1. ESSENTIALS

Dear reader, you are holding the book Basketball Stories. Of course, you were trying hard to find a good book. I hope you will learn something new from it. But you should know that the very first book was written in 1894 by James Naismith and Luther Gulick. Its name was "Basket Ball."

Let's dive into history.

WHEN AND WHY IS THE BASKET?

...it just goes to show what you can do if you have to.
– James Naismith

It was a cold winter in New England back in 1891. Luther Gulick, the head of the physical education department at Springfield College, got an idea. He wanted to fill the gap between football and baseball seasons by having some indoor activity to keep athletes in shape. Mr. Gulick asked James Naismith, a physical educator, to create a new game. This story is well-known, yet its deeper inspiration remains untold. James Naismith was driven by the college's philosophy of spirit (emotions), mind (intelligence), and body (physical health). He invented a game that not only met this challenge but also embodied these values till nowadays. His commitment to these ideals led to the creation of the Basket Ball Game. This game quickly became popular outside college campuses, spreading across New England and around the world, touching millions of lives of all ages.

So, what did it look like, and where did the inspiration come from?

The idea was to cross rugby, lacrosse, soccer, and the childhood game "Duck on a Rock."

Mr. Naismith had a class of eighteen students. He split them into two teams, each with nine eager players, and began to teach them the magical new game he had invented. The goal of this game was to throw a ball into fruit baskets attached to the lower railing of the gym balcony. Whenever someone scored a point, the game paused, and the friendly janitor of the college would bring out a tall ladder to fetch the ball from the basket. Later, to keep the fun going without interruptions, the bottom parts of the fruit baskets were removed, allowing the ball to drop right through. And just like that, the game of basketball was created, bringing joy and excitement to all who played.

Naismith created the first set of 13 rules, outlining the ball's movement and the nature of fouls. The referee was chosen, and the game flow was divided into two 15-minute halves with a 5-minute break in between. The gym class gathered, and selected teams showed the first game of "Basket Ball" on 11 March 1892.

If we suppose Mr. Naismith is a father of basketball, Sarah Berenson can be considered as a mother of this game. Whispers about the new game quickly spread around and came to Smith College. The mother was inspired by the new game and, in no time, went to a father of basketball to get details. Girls during that period were not allowed to participate in activities typically reserved for boys. Sarah Berenson put in a great deal of effort to bring about this change and got acceptance from the community. As you can see, working hard can make any dream come true. After 11 months, the very first women's basketball game took place.

Later, Luther Gulick became the "Basket Ball" brand ambassador and spread the game to a national and international level.

The grand transformation happened in 1906. Metal hoops, nets, and solid backboards appeared, enhancing the game, and making it even more spectacular for players and the audience. This change marked a new chapter in basketball's evolution.

What comes next?

It was spreading faster than you can imagine.

In 1936, a historical event happened. The basketball tournament was organized at the major world contest — the Olympic Games. The games were played on unusual basketball floors — outdoor tennis courts. This momentous occasion marked the beginning of basketball's journey in the world of the Olympics, adding a new and exciting chapter to its never-ending tale.

What about the ball? Was it like nowadays?

Not really. As you remember, the creator of basketball was inspired by various games, including soccer, so the ball comes from it. So, since the very first day of basketball invention, everyone has played basketball with a soccer ball.

Three years later, in 1894, Mr. Naismith decided that the old soccer ball was not performing as he wanted in his wonderful new game. So, he reached out to the famous Spalding company and asked them to create a custom basketball ball. And so, a brand-new ball was created, specifically designed for one of the best games in the world.

Let's return to the quote at the beginning of this story. Remember, if you have an idea – work on it. It can become the next big thing. So, let's answer together:

– When did it happen? – It happened over 130 years ago.

– Why is a basket? – Because at the very start, players should hit the ball into the peach basket.

3-POINT LINE BIRTHDAY

The 3-point shot has created a situation in the game akin to 'Lotto' fever.
— Kareem Abdul-Jabbar

Believe me, the 3-point line is one of the most controversial events in basketball history. The disputes were concerning the distance from where to draw a line. Many people thought it would be the end of the tall players' era. There were more than five attempts to implement it. Here, you will read about some of them.

In 1945, colleges made out the 3-point line and tested it in a game between Columbia and Fordham using a 21-foot line, but it didn't become a rule.

Another test occurred in 1958 with a 23-foot line during a game between St. Francis (NY) and Siena.

In 1961, Boston University and Dartmouth played a game where all field goals counted as three points.

In 1962, St. Francis (NY) coach Daniel Lynch suggested the 3-point line again.

The American Basketball League (ABL) was the first league to use the 3-point line in 1961, thanks to commissioner Abe Saperstein. He wanted to make the game more exciting and different from the NBA. Saperstein believed the 3-pointer could be like a home run in basketball. "We need a special feature," he said, "and this is ours."

One day in the American Basketball Association (ABA) league, the Indiana Pacers trailed 118-116 to the Dallas Chaparrals with just one second remaining on November 13, 1967. Jerry Harkness received the inbound pass 92 feet away from the basket, hurling a high arching shot toward the hoop without wasting time. The ball hit the backboard and went in. There was chaos in Dallas but for an unexpected reason. It was the year 1967 when the top leagues started to adopt a 3-point line. This new rule was unfamiliar to the players and fans. Many of the 2,500 people in attendance that day thought that Harkness' incredible shot had tied the game, anticipating overtime. However, Harkness had taken his shot from 68 feet behind the new 3-point line, bringing the Pacers to a 119-118 win. "We were heading off the court to get ready for overtime when the referee, Joe Belmont, approached me and said

'Jerry, it's over. That was a 3-pointer,'"recounted Harkness in the book "Loose Balls." "I replied, 'I completely forgot about that. A 3-pointer.' We celebrated once more after realizing that we had won the game."

The NBA league introduced the 3-point line in the 1979-80 season.

The first NBA player who hit a 3-pointer was Chris Ford from the Boston Celtics on October 12, 1979. The NBA took some time to adopt the line. In 1980 NBA Finals Game 3, Julius Erving made a historic 3-point shot, marking the first time this happened in Finals history. In Game four, neither team took any shots from beyond the three. In 1988, Danny Ainge was the first to make over 100 3-pointers in a season. He made a record of 148 behind-the-arc shots that year.

Michael Jordan shows how working hard and getting better can lead to success. When he played basketball in college, there was no 3-point line. Michael only made 9 out of 52 attempts in his first year with the Chicago Bulls. It wasn't until his fifth season in the NBA that he got better at shooting from far away. But he kept practicing and improving, and by the end of his time with the Bulls, he was making more than 35 percent of his 3-point shots.

Previously, players spent more time and effort near the basket; now, even big men make long-range shots or even take step-back threes. Centers evolved from powerful and slow players to skinny and quick athletes competing with point guards in skills challenges on NBA All-Star weekends.

In today's NBA, players try a lot of 3-point shots. One player who stands out is Stephen Curry. When he first joined the Golden State Warriors, people already knew he was a good shooter, but he worked hard to improve. Over the years, Curry has broken many records for the most 3-point shots made in a season. He practices shooting from a long distance daily, inspiring many other players to do the same. It's common to see players making their shots from far beyond the arc, changing the gameplay.

After introducing the 3-point line, teams started with 2,8 attempts per season, while modern teams make nearly 35 attempts.

The chart below shows the growing quantity of 3-point shot attempts over at least 20 years.

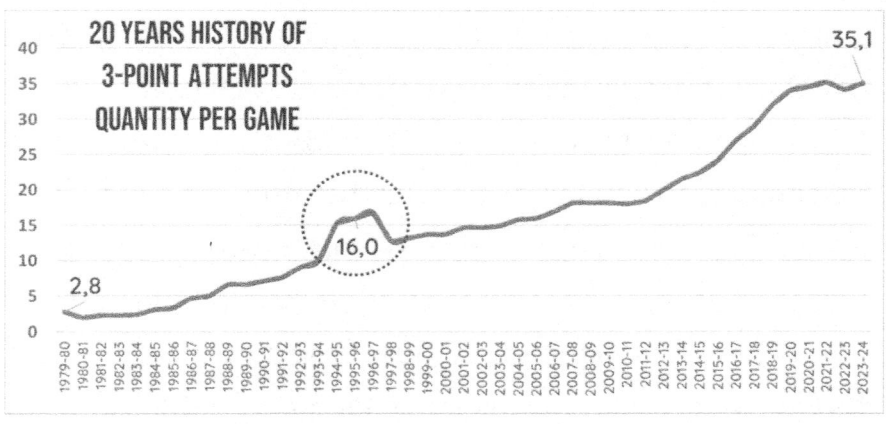

As you can see from the graph above, the number of 3-point shot attempts grows each year. And, if you are curious about what exactly caused that splash in the circle, here is the answer. In these 3 seasons starting from 1994–95 season, the 3-point line was shortened from 23 ft 9 in to 22 ft around the basket. And in 1997–98 season distance was returned to 23 ft 9 in back.

BASKETBALL LANGUAGE

We are unselfish and we trust each other.
—Tim Duncan

One of the indicators of a good player is his familiarity with basketball terminology. Sometimes, outstanding professionals define new terms. A player needs to understand basketball vocabulary for a variety of reasons. Understanding the terminology helps effectively communicate with teammates and coaches during games and practices. Actions and strategies in basketball, such as "pick-and-roll," "zone defense," and "fast break," require a clear understanding and proper execution from all team members. This familiarity makes it easier for players to learn the game and execute strategies and tactics correctly. Coaches typically use specific phrases when providing instructions or feedback. If players are familiar with these terms, it can be easier to understand and follow the coach's instructions, which excludes confusion and mistakes during the game.

When everyone is on the same page with their basketball language, it helps improve teamwork and coordination. Players better communicate, which is crucial in a fast-paced game where split-second decisions can have an impact. As players advance in their basketball careers, they encounter more complex strategies and concepts.

Basketball Dictionary

A

Airball: a shot that doesn't hit the rim, net, or backboard.

Alley-Oop: this is a combination of a pass and a player who jumps to catch the pass and, while hanging in the air, puts the ball into the basket or makes a lay-up.

And One: when a player gets fouled while shooting, and the ball goes in. The player then gets one free throw.

Assist: when a player passes the ball to his teammate who scores after receiving the pass.

B

Backboard: the rectangular flat surface to which the rim is attached. It is often made of wooden board or plastic.

Backdoor cut: it is an offensive move when a player without the ball sprints behind a defender in the direction of the basket.

Bank Shot: a shot when the ball bounces off the backboard and goes to the rim.

Block (action): it is a play when a defender kicks out a shot attempt with his hand, disrupting an offensive attempt.

Block (court area): the area outside the key, where the rectangular blocks are painted.

Box Out: a defensive play when a ball is in the air after a shot. The defender widens his stance and arms, using his body as a barrier, not allowing his opponent to get a rebound. This technique allows a player to secure a rebound.

C

Carry: this violation happens when a player puts his hand under the basketball while dribbling, stops dribbling for a moment, and then starts dribbling again.

Charge: this penalty occurs when an offensive player runs into a standing defender and knocks him over.

D

Double-double: a statistic in a single game when a player gets ten or more points in two categories: points, rebounds, assists, steals, and blocks.

Double Dribble: this call happens when a player dribbles the ball with both hands or dribbles again after taking the ball with two hands.

E

Elbow: the court area where the lane line intersects with the free-throw line.

Euro Step: it is a move when an offensive player picks up his dribble, takes a step in one direction, and then a second step in another direction.

F

Fast Break: it is an action when an offensive team moves the ball and tries to score as quickly as possible. More often, it happens after a defensive action (steal or block) or a missed shot.

Flop: an attempt to draw a foul on an opposing player by acting, simulating, or overdrawing the contact.

Free Throw: a free shot attempt by a player after receiving a foul or a technical foul. The player shoots from the 15-foot free-throw line while others stand outside of the key.

K

Key: the painted area that makes up the free-throw line. It is also called "paint."

L

Lay-Up: a shot taken close to the hoop, usually when a player moves towards the rim.

M

Man-to-Man: this Is a defensive strategy in which each defender guards a player from the opposite team.

O

Outlet: an offensive action when a player who gets a defensive rebound makes a long pass to a teammate for a fast break opportunity.

P

Paint (key): the painted area that makes up the free throw lane.

Pick and Pop: is similar to Pick and Roll, but a player who sets a screen instead of rolling down pops up to the midrange or 3-point area.

Pick and Roll: it is an offensive interaction between the players. One player sets a screen while the player with the ball accepts or denies it. The player who sets a screen then rolls down toward the basket, expecting a possible pass.

Post (block): the area outside of the key in which the rectangular blocks are painted.

Press: this is a defensive strategy when the defenders guard the opposing team more intensively instead of waiting on the opposite side for the offense to come across. The press could be full-court or half-court.

Post Up: an offensive action in which a player gets the ball near the post area with his or her back to the basket.

Putback: when an offensive player gets an offensive rebound and makes a field goal near the basket.

R

Rebound: this is an action when a player gets the ball after a missed shot attempt.

S

Screen: an offensive action when a player without the ball blocks a defensive player to free up a teammate. A screener should remain stationary during the contact, or a moving "screen" will be called, resulting in an offensive foul and a turnover.

Swish: a made shot when the ball touches nothing but the net, avoiding the rim or backboard contact and creating a "swish" sound.

T

Three in the Key: a violation occurs when an offensive player stands inside the painted area (the key) for three seconds or more. It is also called a three-second violation.

Travel: a penalty when an offensive player moves or drags his pivot foot or takes three or more steps without making a cribble.

Triple-double: a statistic in a single game when a player gets ten or more points in three categories: points, rebounds, assists, steals, and blocks.

Turnover: a result of rules violation (foul or out-of-bounds) or defensive action of the opponent (steal) when the offensive team wastes possession.

W

Wingspan: the distance between the left and right fingertips when an athlete extends both arms perpendicular to his body.

Z

Zone Defense: a defensive strategy when players control a specific zone or area of the court instead of a particular player on the opposing team.

A solid understanding of basketball terminology is crucial for building a strong knowledge foundation, which helps to progress, improve at the game, and simply feel confident.

This list consists of the most commonly used practices. Growing up, you will encounter new definitions, and maybe someday you'll invent your own.

IT'S NOT ONLY ABOUT THE SHOES

It's not about the shoes, it's about what you do in them.
— Michael Jordan

In this story, you will learn the history of basketball shoes, their meaning to basketball players as kids and stars, and whether there were any shoes before Air Jordan.

Let's find out the reply to the last question. The answer is YES. But let's first read about the history of basketball shoes and which signature shoes exist a bit later.

History of basketball shoes

You know how fast and traumatic basketball can be, especially if you have slippery shoes. So, players needed some non-slip invention.

The story of specific basketball shoes and their development goes back to 1917. The Converse Rubber Shoe Company set out to design the very first shoes specifically for basketball games. They named the first line the "Non-Skid."

The shoe was a high-top wonder with a sturdy canvas upper and durable rubber sole. Inside, it had a cushioned insole and support for the arch and heel, ensuring comfort for those who wore it. The most enchanting feature was the diamond tread pattern on the sole, which provided extra grip on the floor, allowing players to move confidently.

Later, Converse hired semi-professional basketball player – Charles Taylor as a salesman. Charles made a significant impact on shoe development, advising the improvement of the flexibility of the sole and providing increased support for the ankle. Converse used his idea and released "Chuck Taylor All Stars." It was a huge success. Many basketball players had them on their feet. After the Olympic games, these shoes became famous around the world.

It lasted perfectly for the Converse company until 1958 when the first signature shoes appeared with a real NBA star – Boston Celtics point guard Bob Cousy. Those were "PF Flyers" shoes, now known as "New Balance."

They had canvas uppers, vulcanized rubber soles, and a signature of a famous player on the ankle. The sole print changed to "Circle Grip," which you can find on some Air Jordan models nowadays. New Balance sneakers were so desired that for the first year after release, people bought 14 million pairs. The next model appeared 13 years later.

You will read something special now. You know the brands Adidas and Puma, don't you?

So here it is. These two companies were founded by brothers Adolf (Adi) and Rudolf Dasslers. Both were on a path of creating sports shoes.

Adidas signed a contract with the famous Kareem Abdul-Jabbar. The unique design added a signature of the player and a face visual with his wide smile. This collaboration with the future Hall of Fame spread the famous three-striped print of Adidas worldwide.

Puma also wanted to create basketball shoes and signed a contract with Walt Clyde Frazier. But this pair became more famous off the court as the best hip-hop sneaker. Puma's recognizable wave print on the side of those shoes still exists.

Adidas and Puma were successful in different areas, so Converse wanted revenge. In 1976, they teamed up with Julius Erving and created Dr. J Pro Leather. The shoes were so comfortable that many players could not play in other brands after trying them on.

Finally, in 1985, it was Nike's turn to find a player to represent Nike in the basketball world. Their choice fell on a rookie – Michael Jordan. It was risky enough for a rising brand to sign a contract with such a young player. No one knew how Michael would perform, but Nike realized that if they did not sign Michael, someone else would.

It turned out to be a revolution in basketball shoe history. NBA had a strict rule that shoe color must be 51% of white color. Air Jordans had three colors – white, black, and red (Chicago Bulls colors). So, every time Michael Jordan played in these sneakers, the NBA fined Michael for $5.000, and the Nike company covered all expenses. A new era of colorful basketball shoes started.

Signature shoes and their meaning

Signature shoes are unique sneakers made for and promoted by famous players. These shoes show the player's style and personality and are sold as top-quality brands with individual designs and colors. Nowadays, signature shoes are created not only for performance on the court but also for making a fashion statement off the court.

Now let's speak about the meaning of signature shoes to different people who wear them.

For an NBA player, signature shoes are a chance to leverage his popularity, make more money, and leave a mark in history.

For kids, it is like magic. If you have a pair of your favorite player's signature shoes on your feet, you feel unstoppable on the court; you jump higher like Wemby, run faster ike Westbrook, and shoot threes like Curry.

Many fans collect different models and colors, combining them with various dressing styles and even using them in house designs. Basketball brands like Nike, Jordan, Adidas, Under Armour, Puma, New Balance, Anta, and Li-Ning team up with famous players to create unique shoes. Those shoes have individual designs and match each player's way of playing. Players and fans love them!

Below, you will find an existing list of signature shoes.

Nike is the most famous and worn brand among NBA players (about 67% of players wear it).

The players who signed contracts with Nike are Michael Jordan, Kobe Bryant, LeBron James, Kyrie Irving, Kevin Durant, Paul George, Giannis Antetekoumpo, Ja Morant, Devin Booker, Gary Payton, Scottie Pippen, Charles Barkley, Vince Carter, Jason Kidd, Steve Nash, Dennis Rodman, and Penny Hardaway.

The **Air Jordan** line was so successful that in 1997, Michael Jordan and Nike introduced the Jordan brand. Nike produces it, but Jordan has its own brand and logo. Also, the Jordan brand can sign contracts with NBA players such as Chris Paul, Russell Westbrook, Zion Williamson, Luka Doncic, Jayson Tatum, Dwyane Wade, Carmelo Anthony, Ray Allen, and Rui Hachimura.

Adidas has contracts with such NBA stars as Anthony Edwards, James Harden, Damian Lillard, Donovan Mitchell, Trae Young, Derrick Rose, Kareem Abdul-Jabbar, Tracy McGrady, and Nick Young.

Under Armour: Stephen Curry, De'Aaron Fox, Joel Embiid.

New Balance: Kawhi Leonard, Darius Bazley, Jamal Murray, Dejounte Murray, Zach LaVine, Tyrese Maxey.

Li-Ning: Jimmy Butler, CJ McCollum, Baron Davis, Shaquille O'Neal, Damon Jones, José Calderón, Dwyane Wade, Evan Turner.

Puma: LaMelo Ball, R.J. Barrett, Michael Porter Jr., Marcus Smart, Scoot Henderson.

Anta: Klay Thompson, Gordan Hayward, Kevon Looney, Daniel Gafford, Precious Achiuwa, Rajon Rondo, Kyrie Irving, Kevin Garnett, Donte DiVincenzo

Peak: Lou Williams, Tony Parker, Andrew Wiggins, O.J. Mayo, Nick Young, Dwight Howard, Jose Alvarado.

Since the world of shoe contracts is highly dynamic, some agreements may expire, prompting players to have new deals with other companies.

JUMPMAN LOGO

... it was a ballet move where I jumped up and spread my legs. And I was holding the ball in my left hand.
— Michael Jordan

Michael Jordan's Jumpman logo is one of the most famous symbols in the world of sports. But where did the idea come from?

Before Michael Jordan played his first game in Chicago or even wore Nike shoes, he had a fantastic college career and joined Team USA for the 1984 Olympic Games. During the Olympic training sessions, Michael did a photo shoot for LIFE Magazine; he was wearing New Balance basketball shoes that day. In one photo, he made a remarkable jump.

Next year, while choosing a logo for the Air Jordan brand, Nike decided to repeat that jump photo in their outfit. Michael did another photo shoot with Nike to promote the Air Jordan 1 shoes. This time, he wore the

"Black Toe" Air Jordan 1 shoes and a red and black Nike Air Jordan Flight Suit. With the Chicago skyline in the background, Michael jumped and made the famous Jumpman pose.

Michael once said, "*I wasn't even dunking on that one. People think that I was. I just stood on the floor, jumped up, and spread my legs, and they took the picture. I wasn't even running. Everyone thought I did that by running and taking off. Actually, it was a ballet move where I jumped up and spread my legs. And I was holding the ball in my left hand.*"

True sneaker fans know that the Jumpman logo first appeared on the Air Jordan 3 model.

The first two Air Jordan shoes had a different logo, the Air Jordan Wings logo, created by designers Peter Moore and Bruce Kilgore. However, a photo of Michael's Jumpman pose was used on a hangtag for the Air Jordan 1, marking the first time Nike technically used the Jumpman logo.

Later, Tinker Hatfield, an architect and new shoe designer, saw the photo of the Jumpman pose and had an idea. He decided to use it as the logo for the new model.

The Air Jordan 3 was unique. It was the first mid-cut basketball shoe, the first to use an elephant print texture, and the first to show Nike's Air cushioning as a visible element. It was the first shoe to feature the Jumpman logo on its tongue.

Thirty years later, with many more Air Jordan shoes, the Jumpman logo remains famous. Jumpman transitioned from sneakers to clothes, covering everything from head to toe, including training outfits and outdoor jackets. The logo has remained the same over the years and continues to grow in popularity. People draw the Jumpman logo everywhere, even on backboards and courts. The logo became a symbol. It is recognizable in every part of the world, and when you see it, you know that it means basketball!

THE GREATEST OF ALL TIME

I can accept failure; everyone fails at something. But I can´t accept not trying.
— Michael Jordan

The term GOAT is an abbreviation of "Greatest of All Time." It is used to describe individuals who are considered the best in their field or sport, having achieved an unparalleled level of success and excellence.

There are no clear criteria for defining a GOAT. Every generation can have an idol they have witnessed and believe is the greatest. For older people, the GOAT is Larry Bird or Magic Johnson; for others, it could be Michael Jordan. For younger generations, it's LeBron James or Stephen Curry.

However, some great players have admitted that comparing players from different eras is wrong. But if we really want to define our GOAT, we need to weigh all the facts. Let's try to figure out who could be such a person and whether he fits the GOAT criteria.

For example, we can check current NBA players' opinions. The Athletic Journal (sports department of The New York Times) surveys current NBA players almost annually. They have many different questions, one of them being who the GOAT is. For the third time in a row, the winner is Michael Jordan:

2019 (the first time The Athletic conducted the poll): Jordan earned 73 percent of the votes, with James second at 11.9 percent (a gap of 61.1 percentage points)

2023: Jordan earned 58.3 percent of the votes, with James second at 33 percent (a gap of 25.3 percent)

2024: Jordan earned 45.9 percent of the votes, with James second at 42.1 percent (a gap of just 3.8 percent)

The following are Kobe Bryant, Stephen Curry, and Magic Johnson.

It was a statistic of what players think and who they voted. Let's go deeper and try to define our criteria.

What does it mean to be the best basketball player of all time? Is it to win a championship? How many championships do you need to have to be a GOAT? Should he have an MVP trophy or be the best scorer in the league? Maybe he should be a great defender. Can he be the best in all parts of basketball? I think not. You can dominate in some parts of the game but can't be everywhere on the court. That is why you have a team to help you. Someone has the size to get rebounds easier or has the mass to shove centers near the basket. There are a lot of great shooters, but their defense is not the best, or at least they need help guarding some physical players. That is why every team has different players with different skills, sizes, and roles.

For example, Bill Russel had 11 championship rings. I believe you have heard of Bill Russel and his career. If not, you will have a chance to read about him later in this book. But do you know who Sam Jones is? With ten champion rings, is he better than Michael Jordan, who has six rings? Or did Robert Horry, with seven rings, bring enough effort to help his team win? Or he was lucky to be right there at a specific time when the team was almost ready to win it all but needed the right piece. There is a group of players who have won championships with three different teams: Robert Horry, John Salley, LeBron James, and Danny Green. How good are they? What is their contribution to those wins? Did Danny Grean put enough to the table compared to LeBron James? Can we measure it?

Let's make a list of achievements. We can conclude that GOAT athletes can't be judged by one or a few criteria. The more you have, the bigger your chances of being a GOAT. Of course, you can have your list, or maybe you already know your hero, and any formula can't change your mind.

So, here is the must-have list of accomplishments to be a GOAT:

1. Champion – a key factor. You can't be the greatest if you don't win it (20 points).

2. Hall of Fame – solid indicator. If you have this honor, it means you have already been evaluated (50 points).

3. Finals MVP – this trophy goes to the most valuable player on the court during the finals win (30 points).

4. Season MVP – shows how valuable a player is for his team (10 points).

5. All-NBA team – sportswriters and broadcasters vote for these nominations (first team 8 points, second – 6 points, and third – 4 points).

6. All-Defensive First Team – votes go from head coaches (7 points).

7. All-Defensive Second Team – head coaches' voting (5 points).

8. All-Star selection – the starting lineup for each squad is selected by a combination of fans, players, and media representatives. NBA coaches select reserves (5 points).

9. Scoring champion – if a player is a league leader in average quantity of points per game (6 points).

10. DPOY – defensive player of the year (7 points).

Based on the main accomplishments, we can receive a list of top-5 players:

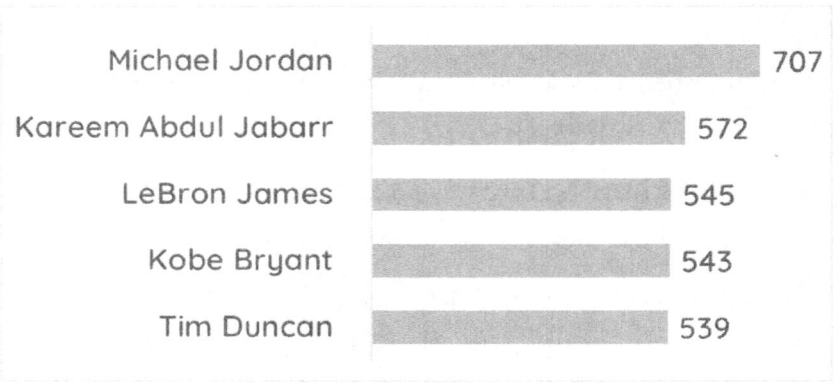

Bill Russel, with 459 points, is worth mentioning as the GOAT. There were no nominations for Defensive Player of the Year or All-Defense First and Second teams when he played. With these nominations, he easily hits the starting five.

As you can see, many factors could be involved in a dispute over a GOAT, such as leaders in blocks, assists, rebounds, or a 3-point or slam-dunk champion.

You can define your criteria and check who is your GOAT.

NBA NICKNAMES

NBA nicknames are like superhero names that players get because of how they play, how they look, their personalities, or epic moments in their careers. It allows to call a player with a short name and in some specific way. Here are some of the awesome NBA nicknames:

A

Kareem Abdul-Jabbar – "The Captain," "A"

Giannis Antetokounmpo – "Greek Freak," "The Alphabet"

B

Charles Barkley – "Chuck," "The Round Mound of Rebound," "Sir Charles," "Prince"

Larry Bird – "The Great White Hope," "The Hick from French Lick," "Larry Legend," "Uncle Larry"

Devin Booker – "Book," "D-Book"

Kobe Bryant – "Black Mamba," "KB-24," "Vino"

Jimmy Butler – "Jimmy Buckets," "Jimmy Jordan"

C

Vince Carter – "Vinsanity," "Old Man Vince," "Air Canada," "Half Man Half Amazing," "VC"

Wilt Chamberlain – "Wilt the Stilt," "The Big Dipper"

Stephen Curry – "Splash Brothers," "Baby-Faced Assassin," "Chef Curry," "Steph," "The Golden Boy"

D

Anthony Davis "Brow," "AD," "Glass," "Day-to-day Davis"

Luka Dončić – "Luka Magic," "Devin Booker's father"

Tim Duncan – "The Big Fundamental," "Slam Duncan," "Old Man"

Kevin Durant – "KD," "Durantula," "The Servant," "Slim Reaper," "Easy Money Sniper," "Snake"

E

Anthony Edwards – "Ant-Man," "Ant"

Joel Embiid – "The Process"

Julius Erving – "Dr. J," "The Doctor"

G

Kevin Garnett – "Big Ticket," "KG," "The Kid"

Paul George – "PG-13," "Young Trece," "Playoff P," "Pandemic P"

Rudy Gobert – "The Stifle Tower"

H

James Harden – "The Beard," "El Chapo"

I

Kyrie Irving – "Uncle Drew," "Kyriediculous," "The Ankletaker"

Allen Iverson – "A.I.," "The Answer," "Bubba Chuck," "Steven John Ray the Third"

J

LeBron James – "The King," "King James," "(The) L-Train," "LBJ" "The Chosen One," "The Akron Hammer," "Bron Bron"

Earvin Johnson – "Magic," "Buck," "E.J."

Nikola Jokić – "Joker"

Michael Jordan – "Air Jordan," "His Airness," "MJ," "The G.O.A.T," "The Black Cat"

L

Kawhi Leonard – "The Claw," "Sugar K"

Damian Lillard – "Dame Dolla," "Sub Zero," "Logo Lillard," "Dame Time"

M

Karl Malone – "The Mailman"

Tracy McGrady – "Sleepy," "T-Mac"

Donovan Mitchell – "Spida"

Ja Morant – "G12," "Ja Warrant"

N

Dirk Nowitzki – "Tall Baller From the G," "Dirty," "The German Racecar," "Bavarian Bomber," "Dirk Diggler," "The Berlin Tall," "German Wunderkind," "Dirk Savage"

O

Shaquille O'Neal – "Shaq," "Shaq Daddy," "Shaq Fu," "Diesel," "The Big Aristotle," "Superman," "MDE" (Most Dominant Ever), "The Big Maravich," "The Big Fella," "The Big Shaqtus," "Big Shamrock," "Shaq Attack"

Hakeem Olajuwon – "The Dream"

P

Chris Paul – "CP3," "The Point God"

Kristaps Porzingis – "KP," "Unicorn," "Tingus Pingus"

R

David Robinson – "The Admiral"

Derrick Rose – "D-Rose," "Windy City Assassin"

Bill Russell – "Russ"

S

Brian Scalabrine – "The White Mamba"

Pascal Siakam – "Spicy P"

T

Klay Thompson – "Splash Brothers," "Game 6 Klay"

Karl-Anthony Towns – "KAT," "Special-K," "The Big Meow"

W

Dwyane Wade – "D-Wade," "Flash"

Ben Wallace – "Big Ben"

Victor Wembanyama – "Wemby," "Alien"

Y

Trae Young – "Ice Trae"

Yes, this is not a complete list, but it includes the most popular or current players.

These nicknames become a big part of who the players are and how people remember them. Just like superheroes!

CHAPTER 2. INCREDIBLE FACT STORIES

In this chapter, you will find amazing true stories of the most iconic historical moments and players, such as Tracy McGrady, Kobe Bryant, Wilt Chamberlain, Michael Jordan, Scottie Pippen, Dennis Rodman, Bill Russel, Phill Jackson, and more.

13 POINTS IN 33 SECONDS

There's a lot of guys, but the guy that always gave me the most problems, actually, was Tracy McGrady. He had all the skills and all the athleticism, but he was 6'10," and he was really tough to figure out. He could do everything I could, but he was 6'10". He had no weaknesses in his game; he could score from anywhere and defend. He's the hardest player I have ever had to guard.
— Kobe Bryant

The story occurred at the Houston Rockets' homecourt on December 9, 2004, against the solid San Antonio Spurs team. The San Antonio Spurs were known for their great defense and discipline. As the game went on, each team showed that there would not be an easy win. The fight was very close, and no team could break away to feel comfortable. The Houston team had a slight advantage in the first half, but the third quarter was not in their control. The Spurs slowly started to go away, and Houston caught themselves by trailing 10 points with one minute till the end of the game. It seemed like all hopes were lost.

The crowd was quiet, and the air was filled with tension. Suddenly, a spark of determination lit up in Tracy McGrady's eyes. He knew he had to do something extraordinary to save his team. With the clock showing just 59 seconds remaining, Tracy received the ball. He drove from the center of the court to meet the best defender of the opponent's team. Tracy made a quick drive to the right and tried to hit a layup, but multiple defenders surrounded him, and he missed! But due to this drive, Yao Ming could take the offensive rebound and put it back with authority! So now the gap is 8 points and 50 seconds left. Houston needed to stop the opponent to survive. The Spurs quickly inbounded the ball, but the Rockets' defense was relentless. They forced a turnover and another quick two points with less than five seconds! Amazing! The crowd went wild! Cheering and screaming, they wanted some magic to happen this evening! The score is 74-68.

The Spurs coach took a time-out to stop this run and have his players take a breath to concentrate.

The game proceeded after an inbound by the Spurs, and Tracy had to take a foul on Devin Brown to stop the clock. Brown was not a great shooter from the free-throw line and not so experienced; he could miss some shots. Unfortunately, he made both attempts, and the lead is back to 8 points.

With 44 seconds to play, Tracy got the ball and controlled it through the center of the court with high-pressure defense. The play began with a "screen" on the 3-point line, allowing Tracy to catch a rhythm for the long shot, and ... YES, SIR! He connects! The lead was cut to 5 points in two possessions. Now you can leave with it – one more stop!

The ball goes live after inbounding, and the Rockets team needs to foul to stop the clock. Again, Devin Brown is 6-6 from the free-throw line this evening. He makes it both, and again, the Rockets need some magic. The score is 78-71 with 31 seconds left.

In the new attack, Tracy got the ball. This time, there was no full-court pressure, which allowed him to concentrate and analyze the defense setup. He used a brick-wall screen by Yao to switch the guard, and now it was Tim Dunkan who tried to guard him but appeared much slower. Tracy felt separation and a good look for a shot – BANG! Another 3-pointer but with a bonus – Duncan has fouled Tracy, so it's and one! Tracy then stepped to the free-throw line and made the shot, completing a magical four-point play. The score was now 78-75.

Another time out by the Spurs; this was getting dangerous.

With 24 seconds on the clock, it's a one-possession game. But the ball was in the Spurs' hands, and the Rockets needed to make one more stop.

Brent Barry inbounds the ball, passing it to Tony Parker to the Spurs' half to kill some time. Parker drives to the 3-point arc and passes the ball to Devin Brown, who then passes it to Duncan. Duncan got fouled. In the pause when Duncan was preparing his shots, the coach of the Spurs, Greg Popovich, came to Brown and reminded him that it was not a great decision to pass the ball to Tim because Brown had 4-4 from the charity stripe and it was preferable to keep dribbling and receive a foul. But the Spurs were lucky, and Tim hit two shots. The score is 80-75 with 16 seconds to play. Houston coach Jeff Van Gundy takes a time-out to draw some plays and instruct players what to do if the team hits or misses a shot.

In the inbound play, Tracy tried to open; with great defense, he could receive the ball only near the half line. Tracy drove to the right wing, where he had already hit the shot; his confidence got high as he felt success from the previous attempt. McGrady goes up and, despite a good contest, hits another three! Bruce Bowen (the best defender in the Spurs and the 5-time All-Defense First Team) spread his hands as he could do nothing more to contest it better. It was a 2-point game, and 11 seconds left. After the shot, everybody stayed near their players to press the Spurs at inbound play. Houston players were hyped; now they believe a win is almost in their hands. But the Spurs coach called for a time-out to organize his time and break the opponent's passion. The Spurs tried to hold the lead, but their confidence was shaken. They quickly inbounded the ball, but inexperienced Devin Brown slipped, and Tracy stole it away with the speed of a lightning bolt. The clock was ticking down, and the crowd held their breath. With just 1.7 seconds left, Tracy dribbled down the court and, with a leap of faith, launched one final three-pointer. The ball arced high and descended gracefully through the net, giving the Rockets a miraculous 81-80 lead.

The arena exploded with joy. The Rockets had pulled off an impossible victory, and Tracy McGrady had become a hero. His incredible 13 points in 33 seconds saved his team, and this event was captured as one of the most iconic moments in the history of the NBA. From that day on, Tracy is known as the hero who never gave up, no matter how desperate the situation seemed.

Tracy McGrady's heroic feat is told and retold throughout the land, inspiring young basketball players and fans everywhere. They learned that even the most impossible challenges could be overcome with courage, determination, and a never-give-up attitude. And so, the legend of Tracy McGrady, the basketball hero, lived on, reminding everyone that heroes are made in the moments when they refuse to surrender.

THE BLACK MAMBA SHOW

You always have to be on edge. You always have to take every practice, every game, like it is your last.
— Kobe Bean Bryant

The basketball world was stunned on January 22, 2006, when Kobe Bryant defeated the Toronto Raptors with an incredible 81-point performance. No one has approached that accomplishment since that evening.

With a 21-20 record, the Los Angeles Lakers were trying to hold positions in the regular season. The Lakers were going through a difficult time, trying to show they can succeed after trading Shaquille O'Neal to the Miami Heat. Many haters were questioning if Kobe could lead the team by himself to the championship.

The Lakers had recently lost back-to-back games – 13 points to Steve Nash's Phoenix Suns and Mike Bibby's

Sacramento Kings in overtime. Kobe was determined to win this game with Lamar Odom, Smush Parker, Kwame Brown, and Chris.

The Toronto Raptors had young Chris Bosh, Morris Peterson, Matt Bonner, Mike James, and Jalen Rose, who were assigned to guard the "Black Mamba."

With 14 points in the first quarter and the Lakers behind by seven, Kobe looked like he was having a typical workday. Despite his additional 12 points in the second period, the Lakers trailed by 14 points at the half.

Bryant really took off in the second half. With 27 points in the third quarter, he scorched the Raptors, giving the Lakers the advantage. However, Kobe wasn't done. He added spins in the fourth quarter, scoring 28 points to get the victory and raising his legacy in NBA history.

Beyond the stats, Kobe was trying to pull his team up through a difficult season with minimal offensive assistance.

Since then, only three players have hit 70 points in a single game: Devin Booker in 2016, Damian Lillard, and Donovan Mitchell in 2023.

UNBEATABLE 100-POINT RECORD

It is said that good things come to those who wait. I believe that good things come to those who work.
— Wilt Chamberlain

Before the Game

A 7-foot-1 (2.16 m) and 260-pound (120 kg) center, Chamberlain was in his third season in the NBA. He set season scoring records in each of his first two years, with 37.6 and then 38.4 points per game.

The third season was even more productive, as he had 50 points on average per game.

Chamberlain scored 67, 65, and 61 points in three earlier games that week, respectively, giving him a career-record 15 times, scoring 60 or more points.

Unfortunately, the game was not televised, and no video footage was found. There are only audio recordings of the fourth quarter. The NBA was not yet recognized as a major sports league and struggled to compete against college basketball. Attendance at the game was approximately half capacity, and no members of the New York press were present.

On the historic night of March 2, 1962, in Hershey, Pennsylvania, basketball legend Wilt Chamberlain achieved the unimaginable. The Philadelphia Warriors were set to face off against the New York Knicks. No one could have thought this game would go down in history as one of the most outstanding individual performances in sports.

Wilt Chamberlain, known as "The Big Dipper," was already a dominant force in the NBA. He was nearly unstoppable on the court. But on this particular night, Wilt did something that no other player has been able to replicate since – he scored 100 points in one game.

The Game Time

The game began like any other, but Wilt quickly established his dominance. By halftime, he had already scored 41 points, a remarkable result by far. The crowd began to sense that they were witnessing something special. Teammates fed Wilt the ball in every possession, understanding that they were part of a potentially historic moment.

In the second half, Wilt continued his scoring rampage. The New York Knicks tried everything to stop him, from double-teaming to fouling, but nothing worked. Wilt was relentless. The crowd grew more electrified with every basket, and the anticipation built. By the end of the third quarter, Wilt had 69 points.

The fourth quarter was a fight against time. Wilt's teammates made it their mission to get him the ball, and the Warriors' strategy shifted to focus entirely on helping Wilt reach the century mark. The Knicks, despite their best efforts, couldn't hold him. With just a few minutes left in the game, Wilt hit a layup to bring his total to 98 points. The crowd held its breath as the game neared its conclusion.

Finally, with less than a minute to go, Wilt received a pass near the basket. He jumped and released the ball, which sailed through the net, giving him 100 points. The crowd erupted in joy and disbelief. Players and fans stormed the court to congratulate Wilt on his incredible achievement. The final score was 169-147, with the Philadelphia Warriors emerging victorious.

Wilt Chamberlain's 100-point game remains one of the most memorable moments in sports history. Not only did he set a record that has stood the test of time, but he also demonstrated the extraordinary potential of an individual athlete. Wilt's performance that night was more than just a display of skill and athleticism; it was a testament to what can be achieved with determination, talent, and the support of a team.

And so the legend of Wilt Chamberlain's 100-point game lives on, inspiring generations of basketball players and fans to dream big and push the boundaries of what is possible on the court.

72 WIN GAMES IN ONE SEASON

Don't ever underestimate the heart of a champion.
— Rudy Tomjanovich

The 2015–16 Golden State Warriors achieved a historic milestone by finishing the regular season with a 73-9 record, surpassing the previous record set by the 1995-96 Chicago Bulls. Despite their outstanding performance, the Warriors fell short in the Finals. Interestingly, the Warriors' head coach, Steve Kerr, has a notable connection to the 1995-96 Bulls team, having played as a point guard for the Bulls during that era.

The 1995-96 Chicago Bulls season is considered one of the greatest achievements in NBA history. The team, led by Michael Jordan, achieved the 72-10 regular season, culminating in an NBA championship.

Here are the detailed aspects of that historic season. Let's return to the previous year.

The Bulls' season 1994-95 was mediocre, with a 47-35 record. The team was ranked 10th in offense and 2nd in defense rating. Despite Jordan's comeback after his retirement, returning his conditions, and getting to know his new teammates better, the playoffs were upset, as the Bulls lost to the Orlando Magic in the second round.

In the offseason, Bulls' management signed the All-Star forward and rebound specialist Dennis Rodman from the San Antonio Spurs and optimized the roster with other changes.

The Bulls started their 1995-96 season with an astonishing 37-0 record at home, part of a long 44-game winning streak. They also won 33 road games, which was the most in NBA history until the 2015-16 Warriors won 34. The Bulls had the best start with only three losses, going 41-3, including an 18-game winning streak. They were unbeatable in January with a perfect 14-0 record and had a 42-5 record at the All-Star break. The Bulls were the first NBA team ever to win 70 regular-season games, finishing first in their division, conference, and the entire NBA, with an incredible 39-2 home record. They are also the only team in NBA history to win more than 70 games and an NBA title in the same season.

The Bulls had an incredible run in the playoffs. First, they beat the Miami Heat 3-0 in the First Round. Then, they defeated the New York Knicks 4-1 in the second round. Next, they swept the Orlando Magic 4-0 in the Eastern Conference Finals. Finally, they won against the Seattle SuperSonics 4-2 in the 1996 NBA Finals, earning their fourth NBA title in six seasons. The Bulls set a record with the best combined regular and postseason record in NBA history at 87-13.

11 RINGS. TWO ICONS

There are two big names who own 11 rings. The quantity is the same, but the contribution and way of achievement are different. We will start with one of the greatest players in basketball history and then proceed with no less remarkable coach.

Lord of the Rings

Success is a result of consistent practice of winning skills and actions. There is nothing miraculous about the process. There is no luck involved.
— Bill Russel

Bill Russell came from a family of regular workers. He was born on February 12, 1934.

During his early years, Russell struggled to develop his basketball skills. Although he was a good runner and jumper with large hands, he did not understand the game, and the Herbert Hoover Junior High School team cut him. As a freshman at Oakland McClymonds High School, Russell almost failed again; coach George Powles saw his raw athletic potential and encouraged the young man to work on fundamentals.

Everyone admitted Russell's unusual style of defense. Later, Bill said that he studied and memorized other players' moves to prepare for defending against them. He often took Dell Magazines' sports publications to learn opponents' motions.

College recruiters ignored Russell and didn't send any offers. But one day, a recruiter from the University of San Francisco (USF), Harold DeJulio, watched his game. Russell's poor scoring and lack of fundamentals did not impress him. However, he felt the young player possessed a remarkable sense of the game, particularly in high-pressure moments. Hal DeJulio referred Bill to his former university, and Russell accepted the scholarship offer. Sports journalist John Taylor described it as a turning point in his life. Bill realized that basketball was his opportunity to escape poverty.

Russell's talent started to rise in university. His unique combination of size, shot-blocking ability, and agility made him the centerpiece of a USF team that quickly established ominant force in college basketball. He used his e prowess to assist USF in winning the National ,ate Athletic Association (NCAA) 1955 and 1956 titles.

After finishing the USF, Russell qualified for the 1956 NBA draft.

In the draft, Red Auerbach, the Celtics' general manager and head coach, wanted to choose Russell because he thought he would solve the team's issues.

Interestingly, Auerbach relied on a colleague's recommendation as he had never seen Russell play. However, the Celtics had to advance in the selection in order to choose him because another team would indeed select Russell, considering his consecutive NCAA championships. The Rochester Royals (current Sacramento Kings) had the first-round pick. Still, they already had a powerful center and needed an outside scorer. The next team with the second pick was the St. Louis Hawks (Atlanta Hawks), so the Celtics gave center Ed Macauley and the rights to guard-forward Cliff Hagan in exchange for Russell.

Before a rookie season, Russell was the captain of the U.S. men's Olympic basketball team, which participated in the 1956 Summer Olympics. Russel had an opportunity to skip the tournament and play an entire season for the Celtics, but he decided to join the Olympic team.

Under the guidance of head coach Gerald Tucker, Russell played a crucial role in leading the U.S. national basketball team to a gold medal victory in Melbourne. In the final game, they dominated with an 89-55 win, completing an impressive undefeated run of 8-0. The U.S. completely dominated the competition, winning each game with an average of 53.5 points. Russell was the team's top scorer, averaging 14.1 points per game.

In the 1956-57 season, the Boston Celtics had a starting five of future Hall of Famers: Russell at the center position, forwards Heinsohn and Frank Ramsey, and guards Bill Sharman and Bob Cousy.

From the start of Russell's debut, he made a significant impact. Russell was a highly skilled help defender who played a crucial role in the Celtics' unique defensive strategy called "Hey, Bill." Whenever a Celtic player needed extra defensive support, they simply called out for assistance. Russell was incredibly fast, swiftly executing a double team and returning to his position before the opponents could even consider finding an open teammate. He also gained a lot of recognition for his exceptional shot-blocking abilities. Experts even gave his blocks a nickname, referring to them as "Wilsonburgers" because he would forcefully reject the Wilson NBA basketballs right back at the opposing shooters. This ability allowed other Celtics players to play more aggressive defense, knowing Russell would protect the basket if they were outplayed.

The Celtics achieved a championship victory in his rookie year. He emerged as the league's first African American superstar, even though he didn't win the NBA's Rookie of the Year award for missing some games while representing the U.S. in the Melbourne 1956 Olympic Games.

Russell played in 48 games and grabbed the most rebounds in the league, 19.6 per game. At the end of that season, the Celtics had a 44–28 record. It took three games for the Celtics to beat the Syracuse Nationals. Then, they played the St. Louis Hawks in the playoffs, led by Pettit and former Celtic Ed Macauley. The highly competitive series came down to the second overtime, where the Boston Celtics triumphed as NBA Champions with a minimal advantage of 125–123.

In the 1957-58, Boston finished second in the regular season and lost the finals to the St. Louis Hawks 4-2.

After an unsuccessful season, Boston had an astonishing eight championships in a row!

Russell achieved an impressive run by winning 11 NBA titles in 13 years, showcasing his exceptional talent and dominance. No other NBA player has achieved a similar level of success. Russell's Celtics were considered the top team in the NBA.

Here are all of Russel's achievements as a player:

9x NBA champion as a player (1957, 1959–66)

2xNBA champion as a playing coach (1968, 1969)

5x NBA Most Valuable Player (1958, 1961–1963, 1965)

12x NBA All-Star (1958–1969)

NBA All-Star Game MVP (1963)

3x All-NBA First Team (1959, 1963, 1965)

8x All-NBA Second Team (1958, 1960–1962, 1964, 1966–1968)

NBA All-Defensive First Team (1969)

In 1975, Russell was admitted into the Naismith Memorial Basketball Hall of Fame. The following year, he was given the Presidential Medal of Freedom.

Bill Russell stood out in a sport that usually rewards scoring and offensive achievements. He was an impressive player who didn't prioritize scoring goals. Instead, Bill excelled at defense, regaining possession, and, above all, preventing shots. He transformed it into a graceful and athletic form like his fellow athletes who challenged conventional notions of attack. Before he arrived, the Celtics, under the guidance of the exceptional passer Bob Cousy, were a team that took excessive shots and lacked discipline. Bill fixed this issue, causing errors, and Boston quickly regained possession. He also guarded the paint with incredible determination, single-handedly compensating for the Celtics' mismatch. Over time, Russell's style became the team's general attitude.

From 1956 to 1969, the Celtics empire underwent significant transformations, yet Bill Russel remained a constant presence and set the team's objectives and mindset.

Bill Russell was an exceptional basketball player, surpassing all others in his time.

As you can see, you do not need to be the best scorer on the team to become a Hall of Famer. The same goes for talent. Yes, talent is a crucial aspect of being the greatest, but what is more important is how much effort you put in, how consistent you are, and what level of concentration you have on the way to becoming the greatest.

The Greatest Coach of All Time

Wisdom is always an overmatch for strength.
— Phil Jackson

There is another person with a record number of rings. As a former NBA player, he won 2 championships. But most of his rings came as he was a coach. What is unique is that he has been working with two of the greatest players who ever played this game. This person has 11 rings as a coach. Among them, 6 with Michael Jordan and 4 with Kobe Bryan. His name is Phill Jackson.

Phil Jackson, born on September 17, 1945, in Deer Lodge, Montana, is a talented basketball player, coach, and chief executive. Using a unique coaching approach inspired by different philosophies and cultures, he led his teams to an impressive 11 NBA championships.

Jackson grew up in Montana and went to high school in North Dakota, where he had an impressive college basketball career, scoring an average of 27.4 points per game during his senior year. His outstanding performance earned him the prestigious title of All-American. In 1969, the NBA's New York Knicks picked him in the draft. He was known for his long hair and hippie lifestyle, riding a bicycle to home games at Madison Square Garden. He was also in Zen Buddhism and experimented with meditation practices. He wrote about his unconventional life in his memoir Maverick (1975).

As a professional, Jackson faced challenges due to his height and health issues. Despite this, he played a valuable role in the Knicks teams, which won NBA championships in 1970 and 1973. He shared the court with legendary players like Bill Bradley, Walt Frazier, Willis Reed, Dave DeBusschere, Earl Monroe, and Jerry Lucas. Jackson learned valuable basketball principles from Knicks coach Red Holzman. He played for the Knicks until the 1977-78 season and then spent his last two seasons with the New Jersey Nets.

Jackson gained coaching experience with the Albany Patroons of the Continental Basketball Association, guiding them to a championship in 1985.

In 1987, Phill Jackson joined the Chicago Bulls as an assistant coach. Two years later, Jackson replaced Doug Collins as the head coach. He immediately implemented assistant coach Tex Winter's triangle offense. He also used management techniques he learned from Holzman with a team that had the best player, Michael Jordan, and rising star Scottie Pippen. They were great at offense and defense, and Jackson let them explore on defense to cause chaos and get turnovers. The outcome was truly remarkable – six NBA championships with an astonishing two three-peats. First three-peat from 1991 to 1993 and second from 1996 to 1998. The 1995–96 Bulls, with a season record of 72 wins and only 10 losses, helped Jackson to achieve a milestone of winning 200 games faster than any other coach before.

After leaving the Bulls and taking a break from basketball, Jackson returned to coach the Los Angeles Lakers. He had the privilege of coaching another pair of superstars, the towering Shaquille O'Neal and the talented Kobe Bryant. Under Jackson's guidance, the Lakers won three consecutive championships from 2000 to 2002. Jackson took a break from the game once more in 2004 but made a comeback as the Lakers' coach in 2005. He led the Lakers to yet another championship in the 2008-09 NBA season, securing his 10th title as a head coach, the most in league history.

In 2009–10, Jackson won his fifth championship with the Lakers. With a total of 11 titles, he left his position after the 2010–11 NBA season.

In 2014, he became the Knicks' team president. As a coach, Jackson succeeded but struggled to repeat that in his front-office position. During his initial three seasons in New York, there were a few questionable moments, including frequent coaching changes and the team's disappointing performance on the court. In June 2017, Jackson and the Knicks decided to separate ways.

Along with meditation sessions and using aroma sticks to break the losing streak, Jackson often assigned books for his players to read.

Jackson's journey from his hippie days to becoming the respected genius among today's NBA coaches was a remarkable transformation. Jackson bridged cultural differences by symbolizing a significant shift in American values and culture. He was included in the Hall of Fame in 2007, and his exceptional coaching abilities earned him the recognition of being named one of the ten greatest coaches of all time in 1996.

THE MOST UNDERRATED PLAYERS

If you have a dream, chase it no matter what it takes.
— James Harden

The NBA draft remains the primary source of getting new players to the teams. The choice of which player to draft decides operations managers rely on scouts' reports. During the year, scouts repeatedly watch videos of college and high school basketball tournaments and visit high schools to see players' behavior. But despite all this work done, there are a lot of surprises after the draft day.

Overall, the draft can resemble some kind of lottery. You never know if a young talent will progress and be prosperous during the career or vice versa if you miss someone's talent. Let's take a closer look at the players who were chosen far from first places but exceeded all expectations.

Isaiah Thomas was the 60th pick in 2011. Thomas, who was 5-foot-9-inch (1.75 m), was a good point guard with excellent ball handling, court vision, and 3-point shot, but his size and defense skills pushed him away from the top picks. Despite this, he has had a solid career with two All-Star appearances. He had his most notable season with the 2016-17 Boston team, averaging 28.9 points and getting 5th place in MVP voting.

Draymond Green – 35th in 2012. Green is known as one of the best defenders. He led the league in steals and was selected as an All-Defensive Team eight times. He won the 2017 NBA Defensive Player of the Year trophy. Green is a four-time NBA champion, a four-time NBA All-Star, a two-time member of the All-NBA Team, and a two-time Olympic gold medalist.

Tony Parker – 28th pick in 2001. Parker got an invitation to the Spurs' summer camp before the 2001 NBA draft. Coach Gregg Popovich put him up for a 1 on 1 game against Lance Blanks, a Spurs scout and former NBA player. Parker was outplayed by Blanks's physical defense, and Popovich did not want to select Parker. Coach changed his mind and gave Parker a second chance after watching a mix tape of his best plays. Parker played better this time. Parker's name did not come up a lot in the mock drafts, and the Spurs picked the point guard 28th overall on draft day. Parker had a successful career, getting four champion titles. He is a 2007 Finals MVP and six-time All-Star player.

Jimmy Butler – 30th pick in 2011. The scouts saw a well-rounded forward with good spot-up shooting and tough defense in Butler. But they also saw him as a solid role-player with no "great" skill and predicted his selection in the early second round (40+ pick). Butler's working ethic and discipline led him to the 2015 NBA Most Improved Player, the true leader of any team, six-time All-Star, and 2023 All-NBA Second Team.

Rudy Gobert – 27th pick in 2013. He was interesting for scouts because he was tall and had a 7-foot-9 wingspan. They admitted Gobert's agility, coordination, and good instincts for the putback. Combining good defensive instincts, lateral quickness, and length, Gobert had great potential in one-on-one defense and help defense. He also disrupted passing lanes and made reaching the rim difficult for small players.

But scouts were worried about Rudy's limited offensive play and weak upper body. Rudy had poor shooting skills and was predictable in his post-moves. But Gobert overcame doubts and became a three-time All-Star, 4x Defensive Player of the Year, and 7x NBA All-Defensive First Team.

Manu Ginobili – 57th pick in 2009. Ginobili was one of the biggest draft steals in history. Before the Ginobili draft, an international player could be considered draft-worthy only if they dominated other leagues in their country and had significant team accomplishments.

When Ginobili was drafted, he had his first year outside Argentina, in Italy. He helped Viola Reggio fix a second place in Italy's second-tier league.

The Spurs team was among the pioneers who realized that international players shouldn't be evaluated solely by their team's achievements. Scouts should also check players' skills separately and forecast how they could progress.

Manu Ginobil is widely credited with changing the game of basketball by popularizing the euro step move in the NBA. He is regarded as one of the greatest shooting guards and sixth man in the league's history. Manu helped the Spurs to get four championship titles and is a two-time NBA All-Star.

Dennis Rodman – 27th pick in 1986. Rodman was in scouts' journals due to his athletic abilities and unique sensation for rebounds. Rodman was so good at defense that he could guard any position from center to point guard. Rodman had contagious energy, which could charge teammates during the game. Due to a lack of fundamentals, he had limited offensive skills and poor midrange shots. Rodman had a lot of personal issues and problematical working ethics. Nevertheless, he found the right teams and professional coaches who knew how to use his strong sides. Rodman is 5x NBA Champion, 2x All-

Star, 7x NBA All-Defensive First Team, led in rebounds for seven seasons, and was honored as a Hall of Famer in 2011.

Nikola Jokic – 41st in 2014. At that time, there were still many doubts about European players, especially if they scored about 18 points on average in the Serbian League. Despite his personal accolades in the European leagues, most of the scouts did not see Jokic's potential. They admitted mostly his flaws, like "unathletic," "lack of strength," "low lateral speed," and "weak defense."

In the first season, Jokic showed his game and became a starting player for Denver, taking third place in the Rookie of the Year award rally. In the second season, he improved his game and finished second in the 2017 NBA Most Improved Player Award voting. In the 2017-18 season, his stats improved to 18.5 points, 10.7 rebounds and 6.1 assists. He recorded the quickest triple-double in NBA history. It took 14 minutes and 33 seconds. In his fourth season, Jokic was already selected as an NBA All-Star and All-NBA First Team and appeared in the MVP race list.

Jokic's journey in the NBA has been one of continuous improvement and success. He has quickly risen to the top, becoming a champion in 2023, an NBA Finals MVP, a 3-time NBA MVP, a 6-time NBA All-Star, and a 4-time All-NBA First Team member. His achievements are a testament to his talent and dedication to the sport.

UNDRAFTED PLAYERS WHO BECAME CHAMPION

Another day, another opportunity to prove everyone who doubts you wrong.
— Michael Jordan

Every year, 30 NBA teams draft young and skilled players. Many young talents want to become NBA players, but only 60 will be lucky. Not every player is selected, and there can be true talents who leave the draft day without a team, and their dreams to be a part of the NBA remain dreams. You must know it is not the end for them or you if such a situation happens.

Some of these undrafted players have something special. They have talent, hard work, resilience, and a determination to succeed no matter what. When you work hard and improve your game daily, NBA teams admit it and invite you to the team.

There are real examples of such situations, and players had a chance to make a team.

The Strong Ben Wallace

In 1996, Ben was not selected during the draft but didn't give up. He worked hard, and soon everyone knew his name. Ben Wallace became one of the biggest defensive stars in NBA history. In 2004, he played a crucial role for the Detroit Pistons, helping them cement the paint and win a championship. Ben was known for blocking shots, grabbing rebounds, and his fierce defense. He got the Defensive Player of the Year accolade four times in five seasons!

The Brave Bruce "Lee" Bowen

Bruce Bowen was another hero who went undrafted in 1993. But like Ben, Bruce didn't let this stop him. He joined the Spurs and became known for his tough defense and discipline. Bruce helped the Spurs win three championships in 2003, 2005, and 2007. He was a valuable puzzle to their success and showed everyone that hard work pays off.

The Determined Avery Johnson

Undrafted in 1988, Avery Johnson found his way to the San Antonio Spell. He was a steady and wise point guard who helped lead his team to victory. In the 1999 championship, Avery made a game-winning shot that sealed their triumph. Later, he became a coach and was named the NBA Coach of the Year in 2006.

The Resilient Udonis Haslem

Then there was Udonis Haslem, who went undrafted in 2002 but joined the Miami Heat and became known for his toughness and reliability. He was a fundamental contributor to the Heat's 2006, 2012, and 2013 championships. Udonis was not only a great player but also a mentor, teaching young players and showing them the way.

The Fearless Fred VanVleet

Fred VanVleet, undrafted in 2016, joined the Toronto Raptors and quickly became a hero. Fred is known for his scoring ability and clutch performances, as he was unbelievable in the Raptors' 2019 championship. His standout play against the Golden State Warriors in the Finals helped his team achieve glory.

The Energetic Jose Juan Barea

Jose Juan Barea, undrafted in 2006, was a vital part of the Dallas Mavericks' 2011 championship team. Known for his energy and playmaking, Jose provided a spark off the bench and played a crucial role in the Mavericks' victory over the Miami Heat in the Finals.

The Tenacious Mike James

Lastly, Mike James, undrafted in 1998, joined the Detroit Pistons. Mike was known for his solid defense and stable shooting. He played valuable minutes off the bench during the Pistons' 2004 championship run, helping his team win.

The journeys of these undrafted players – from being overlooked to becoming champions are the showcase of their dedication, willpower, and ability to seize opportunities and shine. Such stories inspire young players who dream of playing basketball at the highest levels. They are real-life examples of how hard work and determination lead to amazing achievements.

CUT FROM A SCHOOL TEAM BECOMES THE GREATEST

I've failed over and over and over again in my life. And that is why I succeed.
— Michael Jordan

Dear friend, you are on the second story of this book's Motivational Chapter. Please read the next thoroughly. All of us are different in our strengths, mindsets, and beliefs. But if you want to become a great player, it is your time to believe in your dream and work hard, no matter what.

Let's journey back to the high school days of the player who said the quote you just read – Michael Jordan. It happened far before he became a basketball legend.

Picture yourself in future high school. You are entirely passionate about basketball. Constantly practicing, you have been dreaming of making it to the team. The day of the tryouts finally arrives, and your heart is beating as a dribbling ball. You try your best to show your game. But... you don't make it.

Believe it or not, it is the real story of Michael's life. He was just a high school kid with big dreams but faced a crushing disappointment.

Being a sophomore, young Michael eagerly tried out for his varsity basketball team. He was bursting with enthusiasm and dreams of greatness. However, the coaches thought he was too short, skinny, and not skilled enough for this team, so they just rejected him.

This accident could be a devastating blow to his confidence and ambitions. But you should understand that every year, there are a lot of students in the school willing to play, but a team roster has limited capacity. Because of this, coaches pick talents based on their beliefs. Sometimes, they miss true talents. Such situations could happen to anyone. So it is up to you how you react to this situation. You can give up and quit, or you can cry a little (what Michael also did), but then wipe your tears, clench your fists, and work harder to prove they were wrong!

Michael Jordan was frustrated and didn't know what to do. But he received the necessary support from his mother. She said, "If you really want it, you work hard over the summer."[1]

Instead of feeling defeated, Michael used this kick not to fall but to jump forward. This unfortunate event motivated him to practice harder, train longer, and push himself further than ever before.

Years after, in an interview with ESPN, Michael said, "Whenever I was working out and got tired and figured I ought to stop, I'd close my eyes and see that list in the locker room without my name on it."[2]

So, he decided that this situation was not the end of his career, which had not even started yet. Michael showed his play on the junior varsity team.

During that season, Michael didn't just play; he dominated. He scored over 40 points, showcasing his incredible talent and unrestrained drive. This remarkable performance was just the beginning.

This confidence and commitment to follow his dreams set the stage for the incredible journey that would eventually lead him to become a basketball legend, the one who inspires millions.

---

[1] Michael Jordan's mother, Deloris shared it in "The Last Dance" movie, 2022
[2] Interview to ESPN
https://espn.com/sportscentury/features/00016048.html#:~:text=%22Whenever%20I%20was%20working%20out,and%20he%20wanted%20a%20second.

CHAPTER 3. INSPIRATIONAL TALES

And now, I welcome you into the world of amazing adventures and inspiring tales. These tales are filled with exciting journeys and essential lessons that remind us to always believe in ourselves and never give up. Get ready to be inspired and have fun.

INSIDE THE TEAM

You can´t win if you don´t play as a unit.
— Kareem Abdul-Jabbar

Back in the day, in a pretty ordinary school in a small town, there was a basketball team called the Conway Foxes. The team consisted of kids who loved to play basketball. But there was one problem: they needed to learn how to work together as a team.

This new school year, the school hired a new coach named Nail. He noticed that there was no team play right away. During the practice, some children were always eager to shoot the ball, while others were more focused on dribbling and forgot to pass. Also, some of them were confused and did not know what to do with the ball. Coach Nail decided it was time to teach them about the different roles and duties inside the team and the importance of communication between teammates.

"All right, Foxes," coach Nail said, gathering the team in a circle. "Basketball is more than just shooting hoops. Each of you has unique skills, strengths, and advantages. It is essential to showcase your strengths and contribute effectively to the team. How about I tell you about the different roles and positions that you can occupy?

As you already know, there are five positions on the court: point guard, shooting guard, small forward, power forward, and center. I will explain them and tell you who of you will be assigned to which of them."

Coach Nail started with the point guard. "This is the floor general, the one who directs the play. You need to have excellent ball-handling skills and a good understanding of the game. Your job is to bring the ball up the court, set up the offense, and ensure everyone is in the right place."

Jake, who loved to dribble and had quick reflexes, was chosen as the point guard. He felt proud to be trusted with such an important role.

Next, coach Nail described the shooting guar. "This player needs to be sharp, able to shoot from long distances and make quick decisions. You need to move without the ball to get open shots."

Sandy, who had a talent for sinking 3-pointers, was perfect for this position. She loved the idea of being the team's sharpshooter.

"The small forward is a versatile player," coach Nail continued. "You need to be able to shoot, pass, and defend. You must be quick and able to adapt to different situations. It is like a combo in one person."

Bobby, who was good at offense and defense, took on this role. He liked being the all-around player who could do a little bit of everything.

Coach Nail then switched to the power forward. "You need to be powerful and aggressive in a good way, a good rebounder, and score near the basket. You are the one who battles for position and protects the paint."

John, who was tall enough and the strongest, fit this role perfectly. He enjoyed using his strength to help the team.

Coach Nail explained the center's role: "You are the tallest player, and your main job is to block shots, get rebounds, and score the most closely to the basket. Also, you need to be a big presence on defense."

Dany was even taller than John, and the coach chose him as the center. He felt proud to be the team's big defender. He realized that, for real, shooting near the basket is much easier for him than shooting from the 3-point line.

And the most essential thing the coach left for dessert. He finalized a short lesson with the most important thing for a team that makes all positions united. With all the roles assigned, Mr. Nail emphasized that communication is crucial for the team's success. "To be a great team, you must talk to each other. Call out screens, let each other know when you are open, and encourage each other. Remember, you get a win as a team, and you lose as a team. No pointing fingers. Just support."

The Foxes started practicing playing their new roles and focused on communication. They called out teammates, cheered each other, and ensured everyone knew what was happening on the court.

The day of the big game has finally arrived. The Conway Foxes were up against their rivals, the Preston Wolves. They were known for their strong teamwork and skills.

The game was intense, and Foxes showed a completely different level. The prior chaos disappeared, and it was clear that everyone knew what to do. Jake expertly directed the team as the point guard, Sandy hit crucial shots from beyond the arc, Bobby showed solid basketball, Dany dominated the rebounds, and John was a defensive powerhouse.

But the most noticeable for the audience was an improvement in communication. The Foxes constantly talked to each other, and it was visible that everyone was on the same page. They encouraged each other and played as one unit.

In the game's final moment, the score tied. Jake called for a pick-and-roll to pass the ball to Sandy. John set a solid screen. Sandy was open, and the pass came without hesitation. She took the shot and scored, winning the game for the Conway Foxes.

The Foxes celebrated their victory not only because they won but also because they learned the value of teamwork and communication and applied their roles in practice. Coach Nail gathered them in a locker room and said, "I am proud of you and your united game. Support and use of your strengths did the trick."

The Conway Foxes became a tremendous competitive team, won many games, and became big friends. Everyone wanted to join them and be a part of their magic.

They always remembered coach Nail's concepts: in basketball, just like in life, everyone has a role to play, and helping each other makes the game easier.

ROLE MODELS

I´m not a role model... Just because I dunk a basketball doesn´t mean I should raise your kids.
— Charles Barkley

Have you ever heard someone shout a basketball player's name or his known phrases while doing a signature move on the playground? "Kareem Abdul-Jabbar!" during a hook shot, "Michael" or "Kobe" when performing a fadeaway jump shot, or Dikembe Mutombo's "Not in my house" after a blocked shot.

When you play basketball, try to notice your friends' play styles. Someone loves to do a stepback shot, euro step, or celebration after a successful episode. Have you ever felt that you saw these moves before?

You are right. You actually saw it, and it is not a coincidence. Basketball superstars have their signature moves or phrases. If you or some of your friends copy their behavior – it means this particular hooper became a role model.

It's not just you or your friends who admire and impersonate the behavior of a favorite player. It is a common trend among youngsters. They see their idols on the court and want to be just like them. Chasing a dream of becoming a basketball superstar, young boys copy their role model moves and mannerisms. Of course, each person could have different role models. Some love great shooters, while others prefer defensive players or some creative passes.

Below, you will meet players who are very famous among the fans and regarded as role models.

LeBron James is considered by many fans to be one of the greatest players of all time. His longevity, dominance, and success find fans in every country worldwide.

Stephen Curry is well known for his 3-point shooting, as he is not a giant and needs more effort to dominate this league. Luka Doncic or Kyrie Irving – are great point guards who are magicians with the ball and can do whatever they want with their defenders.

Michael Jordan is a role model, even for people who do not play basketball. Through his discipline, he achieved great success, and by quotes and self-examples, he teaches and motivates others to achieve it.

Of course, there are many other role models, and it depends on your preferences in playing style. However, role models do not have to be athletes.

Here is the story of a young boy named Alex.

He enjoyed using a tablet to play games and watch videos, but he also loved basketball more than anything else. Alex would ride his bike to the neighborhood basketball court every day to practice his shots and dribble. His dream was to succeed as a basketball player.

One summer day, while Alex was working on his shot, he saw an older man who came to throw some shots, too. Alex noticed that that man had good handles and a nice jumper. He hit almost all of his shots. The man saw Alex's interest and walked over to him. He said, "Hello, I am coach Carter." "I saw you working out every day. I love what you do, and I believe you have a lot of potential". Alex's eyes widened. "Wow, thanks, coach! I want to be the best player I can be, but I know I still have much to learn." "Well, how about I help you with this? I train the high school basketball team and would happily give you some tips." – coach said.

From that day on, Alex and coach Carter meet at the same place to exercise. After some time, coach Carter invited Alex to his team. He taught Alex not just about basketball but also about life. The coach emphasized the necessity of diligence, self-control, and teamwork. He taught Alex how to improve mentally and be a good sport, whether winning or losing. Coach Carter stated, "Scoring points is not the only aspect of basketball. The key is to work together with your team, show respect for your opponents, read the game, and give everything you can in every single game."

The coach guided Alex to a significant improvement in his game. Alex gained the confidence to shoot, assist with accuracy, and control the ball reliably. But more importantly, he learned how to be a leader on and off the court.

One evening, after intense training, Alex sat down with coach Carter. "Coach, I have learned so much from you. But I'm curious: who was your role model?"

Coach Carter took a moment and smiled thoughtfully. "My role model was my old coach, Taylor. He taught me everything I know. He often reminded me that the greatest players are not just the ones who score the most points; they are the ones who encourage their teammates and never give up". So now I share this knowledge with you." After these words, Alex decided to develop as a team leader.

Alex had a chance to make a game-winning shot in the next big game, but he passed the ball to his friend Max because he was in a better position. Max made the shot, and their team won the game.

Coach Carter praised Alex for his decision: "That was a great pass, Alex. You showed real leadership out there."

Alex grinned proudly. He understood that playing outstanding basketball was not enough; you also needed to help other players use their strength.

Alex grew into a remarkable basketball player and a respected leader. He always remembered the lessons Carter had taught him. The coach shared his knowledge and guided younger players, emphasizing the value of hard work, team connection, and integrity.

The legacy of being a role model continued, passing from generation to generation through the love of basketball and the spirit of competition.

Well, young basketball player, as you see, your coach can also be a role model. You can learn much from your role model or create your own play style, moves, and celebrations. It is important to be true to yourself and discover your personality the way to your dream.

STARTED FROM THE BOTTOM, NOW WE ARE HERE

I grew up poor, but I didn't have poor dreams.
— Magic Johnson

A boy named Jason Will lived in a typical small town that had seen better days. He was born into a poor family, and his childhood was not as lucky and happy as every kid desires.

His father had left a family when he was only two years old, disappearing without a word, leaving behind two kids, a wife, and a pile of unpaid bills.

The abandoned family had no other option except to move to a grandparents' house. The grandmother cared for the kids, while Jason's mother, Lory, worked tirelessly in two jobs to give her children a better life.

Despite her efforts, there was never enough food or money on the table to keep the house warm in winter. The winters in their town were severe. On cold nights, Jason was sitting with his younger sister, Lili, under a stack of blankets, listening to his mother's stories about hope, dreams, and passion. Sometimes, these stories entered his dreams. He saw himself as a grown-up, providing his family with a new house with a solid roof, warm walls, a car, and a full fridge of food.

Every year, Jason was waiting eagerly for autumn. And not because of school, but because of NBA season start. At his grandparents' house, there was an old, flickering TV. Jason was sitting with his grandpa in a large, old but cozy armchair, watching games and listening to the rules of the game Grandpa explained to him. Despite the poor signal, he tried to catch every moment this magical box could give. Jason was excitedly watching how athletic players were flying from one hoop to another as if they were from another planet. Every time, he imagined himself in that box. The crowd was cheering; he was definitely not hungry, the team believed in him, they won the game, and he felt himself at the top of the world

But his rumbling stomach returned dreams to real life. He knew he would search for a basketball team there on the first day of school. He already had a fire in his heart and confidence that there was no other way for him except to become a basketball player.

He was unstoppable. When there was no basketball training at school, he went to the old park downtown to practice and learn new moves. Jason felt that every shot he made and rebound he took brought him closer to the dream.

The hardest part for Jason was education. He did not really love to read or do the math. But the coach told him once, "You have all the necessary skills to be a great player. I see your desire to win. But you need to know that there are no other chances to get where you want except to study well enough to get into college. It will be a bridge for you to way out." Day after day, Jason's average grades and skills rose.

One day, during his freshman year in high school, everything changed. Jason was playing in a local basketball tournament. His passion and skills were evident to everyone who watched the game. Among the spectators was a scout, Sam, from a prestigious college, who accidentally appeared in this town and decided to watch the game. He was enchanted by Jason's talent and unstoppable desire to win. After the match, Sam came to Jason and said, "I am lucky to be at this game today and find you. Now let's check how lucky you are in your grades at school. Wait for me at the entrance". Scout Sam met with a school director and discussed Jason's academic degree. They both came to Jason, and Sam offered a full scholarship at the college. The scout's business card felt like a golden ticket in Jason's hands.

On the way home, tears filled Jason's eyes. He realized that his dream was getting closer.

College life was demanding, but whenever he wanted to whine, he recalled cold childhood nights and roaring stomach, his mom still working two jobs, and his sister who did not have a scholarship yet. These memories helped him proceed with his hard work.

The draft day began. Jason was sitting with his family, feeling himself on the edge. It was the day he had dreamed of for so long. Sweating in expectation, he heard the host pronouncing his name.

It seemed like everyone in this room heard his exhalation. Jason stepped onto the stage. He mentioned every name who helped him on the way to this place: Grandpa's rules explanation, Mom's hard work to buy new sneakers for his never-stop-growing feet, coaches from primary school to college, and himself for his hard work and strong belief in this dream.

Years of hard work paid off. Jason achieved his childhood dreams. He could buy his mom a new house and a car and get his sister to college.

Dear buddy, you need to know Jason's story is not unique. There are many players with similar stories. Among them were Larry Bird and Ben Wallace, who knew the word "poverty" not from the tales. Derrick Rose dreamed of running away from rough living areas. Serge Ibaka is a guy who met war and lived without water.

Abandoned by their father, Jimmy Butler, Kevin Durant, and LeBron James. It is not a complete list of those who know hunger and did not see his mom enough because she worked hard as Jason's mom.

Remember, it does not matter what your status is. What matters is your belief in your dream, belief in yourself, and constant hard work to sharpen your skills.

CHAPTER 4. MOTIVATION CHARGER

Dear reader. You can return to this chapter every time you need motivation. Here, you can find NBA players' famous quotes and encouraging words that will help you overcome obstacles or hard times. Live your life and follow your dreams. Do not forget about teamwork. It is not just a word. There is no "I" letter in the team. Motivate your teammates as you motivate yourself and share your confidence. It will return to you with a good surprise. The following chapters will help you with all of this.

30 MOTIVATIONAL QUOTES

All kids need is a little help, a little hope, and somebody who believes in them.
— Magic Johnson

It is true. But remember, you have not only people who believe in you, but this book also believes in you. Please find motivational quotes from basketball players below.

They have reached their dreams through hard work and have followed their dreams. They love this game, and I believe you too.

Use please next quotes when you feel a little lazy, demotivated, or tired, or for the moment, you think that someone is more talented. As mentioned before, talent is essential for success, but hard work is the most crucial.

"You can't get much done in life if you only work on the days when you feel good." – Jerry West.

"Hard work beats talent when talent fails to work hard." – Kevin Durant.

"When you are not practicing, someone else is getting better." – Allen Iverson.

"The only way to get better at basketball is to put in the work and practice consistently." – Stephen Curry.

"Basketball is a game of discipline and focus. If you´re not focused and disciplined, you´re not going to be successful." – Larry Bird.

"The one thing do that nobody else does is jump three and four times for one rebound." – Dennis Rodman.

"When I play bad, I don't get too down on myself. When I play good, I don't get too hot." – Jayson Tatum.

"Growing up in a trailer, you think everything you get is good. I always thought it was a gift from God because some people are out here struggling and on the street. We had warmth. We had clothes. We had a roof over our head." – Bam Adebayo.

"I know I've got a lot more to learn, so I'm just taking it game by game." – Donovan Mitchell.

The next ones are for teamwork:

"Ask not what your teammates can do for you. Ask what you can do for them." – Magic Johnson.

"Talent wins games, but teamwork and intelligence win championships." – Michael Jordan.

"Basketball is a team game, and the only way to be successful is to work together and trust each other." – Dwayne Wade.

"If I can't score, I do whatever I can to support my teammates." – Giannis Antetokounmpo.

"I can score the basketball, but I think I can pass pretty well, or I can make the correct pass. I'm not the type of guy who's just going to throw the ball inbounds to a guy who's wide open. I can make the right pass." – Kevin Durant.

"The only way to be successful in basketball is to work hard, play together, and trust each other." – Chris Paul.

"This is what real teams do in tough times, is stick together. It's easy to stay together when it's all good, you know? The tough times, that's when you have to stay together." – Luka Doncic.

"What I pride myself on mostly is making the game easier for my teammates." – Rajon Rondo.

If you fail someday, you can read the following quotes to cheer up:

"Success is a result of consistent practice of winning skills and actions. There is nothing miraculous about the process. There is no luck involved." – Bill Russell.

"My whole life, people have doubted me. My mom did. People told me in high school I was too short and not fast enough to play basketball. They didn't know my story. Because if they did, they'd know that anything is possible." – Jimmy Butler.

"I´ve missed more than 9,000 shots in my career. I´ve lost almost 300 games. 26 times, I´ve been trusted to take the game-winning shot and missed. I´ve failed over and over and over again in my life. And that is why I succeed." – Michael Jordan.

"If you´re trying to achieve, there will be roadblocks. I´ve had them; everybody has had them. But obstacles don´t have to stop you. If you run into a wall, don´t turn around and give up. Figure out how to climb it, go through it, or work around it." – Michael Jordan.

"I´ve always felt that I could play basketball, but I just had to work a little harder than the next guy to get it done." – Jason Kidd.

"If you´re afraid to fail, then you´re probably going to fail." – Kobe Bryant.

"Basketball is a game of mental toughness. It´s about being able to stay focused and not getting rattled under pressure." – James Harden.

"The only person who can really motivate you is you." – Shaquille O'Neal.

"If you don't fall, how are you going to know what getting up is like." – Steph Curry.

"It doesn't matter if you fall down, it's whether you get back up." – Michael Jordan.

"Always turn a negative situation into a positive situation." – Michael Jordan.

"You gotta have confidence in yourself first before anybody else will. I've always had that." – Jayson Tatum.

"My dream was bigger than anything else. My fight and me wanting to fulfill what I wanted to be in life. That was enough to keep me strong enough to endure anything." – Allen Iverson.

MOTIVATIONAL MOVIES LIST

People ask me, will I remember them if I make it? I tell them, will you remember me if I don't?
The movie: "Hoop Dreams"

Hey, you already have a full head of essential history. Real-life stories, motivational tales, and quotes from famous players will keep a fire inside you, keeping your belief that dreams come true. Sometimes, there could be hard days when you could question yourself, "Is this really what I want?" Be prepared. It can happen due to someone's careless words, a lost game, or you just being tired from the training.

During these challenging moments, try to recall your inner desire, relax, and concentrate. Your reaction to what is happening is most important.

Someone's critical words. If they are meaningful – take them into account and rise. If they are just disappointing with no sense, then there is no sense to be disappointed.

If you are tired – you already know that those who work hard achieve their dreams.

If you have lost a game, don't blame yourself or anyone; make conclusions and move forward.

If these advice do not help, I've compiled a top list of motivational movies for kids and teens. Watch some of those movies and feel your power again to stay on your path to your dream life.

Here is the list of basketball movies. Some are motivational, and others are just for fun. But before watching, ask your parents for permission, alright?

"**Like Mike**" (2 parts) – fantastic stories about boys who find an old pair of Michael Jordan sneakers and magically start playing like professional players. During their adventures, boys feel that friendship and teamwork are essential in life.

"**Air Bud**" is a story about Josh's friendship with his dog Buddy, who helps his friend through tough times.

"**Space Jam**" (2 parts). These are fun animated comedy movies with two basketball legends as main characters: Michael Jordan and LeBron James. These movies have fantastic plots, but the main idea is that if you believe in something, you can achieve it.

"**Glory Road**" and "**Hoosiers**" are inspiring movies about coaches and their teams. They show how they went from the bottom to national league players. You will find their motivational quotes and a great example of how hard work and teamwork bring you to the top.

Here is also a list of documentary movies:

"**Kobe Doin' Work**" is a film about Kobe's usual day before, during, and right after one game. This movie shows the internal processes of the NBA team and the work attitude of Kobe Bryant.

"**The Last Dance**" is a 10-series documentary film about Michael Jordan's life and the Chicago Bulls' 97-98 season. It also features interviews with many NBA stars.

"**Shooting Stars**" and "**More Than a Game**" are documentaries about LeBron James and his four childhood friends. The movies show how friendship and support made them the best high school team in the town.

"**AIR**" – a documentary movie about the origin of the Air Jordan shoe line. The story revolves around signing the most fabulous shoe contract in history.

"**Rise**" is a documentary about the Antetokounmpo brothers' rough life and path to the NBA.

"**Stephen Curry: Underrated**" is a documentary movie about Stephen Curry's life from his childhood and his desire to prove that size does not matter if you are working hard.

"**Hoop Dreams**" is a real story that has been filmed for five years. It is about two boys struggling to become basketball players in college on the way to their main dream – the NBA.

Of course, many more motivational movies exist, but this list was made for kids and fits the family movie category.

Enjoy.

MY DREAMS

Here you have a place to write down your own dreams. The secret is that dreams like to be written. Then it is easier for them to come true.

NOTES

Here you can write important notes from the book or life. As well as you can write here how you plan to implement your dreams. And it will be your commitment to yourself.

VISION BOARD OF YOUR DREAMS

Here, on a blank page, you can draw or put your stickers, which represent parts of your dreams. And you will have a full picture of your Dream Life. Good luck!

Thank you for purchasing my book, and I hope you enjoyed it as much as I enjoyed writing it.

Your feedback is valuable to me. If you have any questions, suggestions for improvement, or have noticed any errors, kindly ask you to reach out via email:

kevinparkerauthor@gmail.com

As a bonus of my appreciation for your valuable input, I will provide you with a complimentary updated eBook version of this book.

Your participation and feedback are highly valued. Scan the QR code to leave an honest review and help make this book to be noticeable.

Thank you for engaging!

Printed in Great Britain
by Amazon